CW01678091

The Mud is Quiet

The Mud is Quiet

Colin Kerr

Chapman Publications
1993

Published by
Chapman
4 Broughton Place
Edinburgh EH1 3RX
Scotland

The publisher acknowledges the financial assistance of the Scottish Arts Council in the publication of this volume.

A catalogue record for this volume is available from the British Library.
ISBN 0-906772-57-5

Chapman New Writing Series
Editor Joy Hendry
ISSN 0953-5306

Some of these poems, or versions of them, have previously appeared in *Chapman, Firrword, Glasgow Magazine, Graffiti, Malahat Review, Northlight, Open World, Sempervivum, West Coast Magazine* and *Different People* (Straight Line Publications).

Designed & typeset by Peter Cudmore
Cover design by Ruth Addinall

Printed by
Mayfair Printers
Print House
William Street
Sunderland
Tyne and Wear

Contents

Introduction by Valerie Gillies

Preface

Knowledge

Landscapes of mind & place

Introduction

Not content with his first training in electrical engineering, Colin Kerr began to study philosophy. He combines these studies now to produce new poetic possibilities. Always curious, he is looking for other explanations of phenomena. Currently a teacher, he may say to his pupils, "Your homework tonight is to go outside at midnight and look at the stars." And his pupils like it. They can see that he asks questions to which he doesn't already know the answers.

In the same way, he makes poems which are accessible to an intuitive reading. Their questions keep echoing, long after the book is closed.

His interests lie in comparative philosophy, in physics, in electricity and science in general. Taoism, too, begins to emerge in his poem-book, especially the moving meditation of Tai Chi with its accuracy and flowing, turning rhythm.

Along with the Taoist simplicity and the circulation of internal energy, these poems share some other characteristics of Chinese poetry. There are the parallels in imagery and the gaps in punctuation which give space, the rhythms which lend weight to individual words. Language is pared to a minimum where parts of grammar and punctuation are often absent. Where there are no full stops the poem's field of meaning enlarges. The danger for those who mimic oriental structures in English is that the poetry may become flat and simplistic. Open syntax keeps it from monotony. At its best, the minimal language lends immediacy. Reduction as a formal structure leads to balance, a sense of poise.

Such spare language creates reciprocal configurations for experience. While thought is in motion, the poem can begin to move its readers.

This is contemporary work. Favourable comparisons could be made with Alan Spence's *Glasgow Zen* or Kenneth White's *The Bird Path*.

Colin Kerr has gathered poems under helpful headings, dovetailing topic and tone. These gatherings first began to form into clutches when he read them in public: for example, the section entitled 'Time' looks into the past, and sees into the future. 'Landscape and Mind' has its own geomancy, divining configurations of place and our human response. The strategy of 'Integration' combines parts into a whole just as, in electronics, the integrated circuit replaces several separate components.

Colin Kerr loves the old Caledonian forest, and camps near it each year. He has a wish to take care of it, to conserve a few acres of native woods, for the sake of the energy people can enjoy just by being in such a place. His poetry, too, is a continuous growth, its energy is regenerative. There are places where it feels good for us to be, and poetry which it's good for us to read.

Valerie Gillies
July, 1993

Preface

Mother

In your eyes
the green of a dawn

on my far-away horizons

Father

So again we talk   yes knowingly

as if we do

Ancestor – female

Her grey silhouette curves
and turns around
to become a green seabell
suspended
above my ocean floor

There it glides so slowly
from left to right
that its song is heard
from many tides ago

Spreading outwards on each shore
it ripples light
over sand

or in rock pools

reflects far-above   bird circles
beside seaweed

And once ashore
sodden footprints
merge back
into speckled sand

as the music
if it ever existed
returns across the blue distance
of sea swell   as if breathing

and I   put my ear
to this sound mirror
an empty shell

Seabird

His wingtips over waves
dip   and caress
angle toward crest-spray
roll windswept   then breathless
motionless   those rainbows

Low against the water-
-grey hollows
between waves
comes a wingspan
a still movement
head this way   then that

Yellow   a pale yellow
beak searching
for sleek fin trails
darting
beneath slitherings
of wind's surface   upon sea

like images beneath words
among belief
that something happens there
a moment's hung   or passes
but when gulping down through this saltspray
there is no more frightening flesh   alive

The Stranger

Always there sitting beside me
at the table
talking
like a wind urging on
an incoming tide

On the seafront
where I sat
in a bus shelter
waiting
I could hear his every breath

The people in the queue
stood
facing the other way
looking out
towards the town

He was alone
though I asked him
what he felt like eating
Fish, he said
and flew away
by way of another tale

In the space before dessert
I got up
and offered him my chair
It was like
walking on water

I joked with him
that this bus route
he'd be pleased to hear
had already crossed the Red Sea

He looked at me
through his grey mist
covered eyes
I'm grateful   he said
that you have heard these old stories

Then he told me
that the other people
in the bus queue
had simply thought
he was a seagull

The other

The river is black today
and yellow leaves
fall to and fro
onto its surface

Time only seems
to stay at the edges
where a green shoreline
is substantial

and you keep calling me to come
to bring my time
into your time   to come
and float an image up
and down the ripples
of a once and for all passing

By this low bridge
of your surviving
I am like water
off the back
of each reflection

though only your fingers
as you kneel down
have understood

Poet's Image

I see a poet, trying
to create just one more line

becalmed in pools reflecting
what emerges from the rippling mime

a depth-charged image enlightening
as a frog splashes up through my mind

Metaphor

Night falls in his head
between clouds between images
L I G H T n i i i i n g flash

Outside   just a moon
fool circling in awe   of a moment
a moment passed by

A SH H H H H H OOOOOting star
that pulls dream torn messages
across empty space   in thought

Classroom Antics

His chalkdust glove
makes a silent
mime
there on the blackboard

leaving the impression
of learning
in black and white

Whisperings at his back
blow over
this old snowscene

as a breath of wind
across his first
footprints

Quietly now
it seems
he understands nothing
but dust-
-like
crystal
blown figures
on a windowpane

a form of knowledge
through which each
might dimly perceive
an other

and being able
to look there
is the lingering fight
that we share

Dunce

His brain was like two wings
of a white moth

always sucking his body
into the central blaze
of an enlightened mind

Mapmaker

He looks outwards   through me
in a way that seems to turn my existence
into a dream   Pupils
dilate

till there is no more sky blue
Only stars   in this darkness

On this edge of his universe
I must sit
thoughts twinkling
until a course is plotted

for there   are the materials between us
to make a map

Examination

In the hall we awoke
to all that we didn't know

The clocks ticked
past our lives

Doors   didn't open
or close

They disappeared

Losing sight
of all that he knew

he dropped beads of sweat
onto lined paper

to record
his tune

The words followed

Examination II

By the second exam of the week
he had settled in
to the cockpit
of system

Sometimes the controls
worked
by themselves

The instruments always did

As a passenger
he always viewed the world
as one step removed from time

When these exams would allow him
to fly
would never
be up to him

As a pilot he looped the loop
of clockfaces
finding his hands coming together
opposite
all those high noons
of systematic control

As a pilot he put down the answers
as if landing by radar

the wind only being felt
between cockpit
and pilot's lounge

The knowledge that he used
was breathless

Dead

Journeys of Perception

At first it is simply the acknowledgement
of an unknown

as this poem hangs above the page
in the way that black
type-written letters
don't

The poet's job therefore
is to reach up
and pull down that blackness
like a shade

He must cut all those tiny holes
and slits in this darkness
using only his feeling
for fingertip
touch

He is slowly making clear a vision
to bring through the cracked sunlight
in a morning curtain

This will lift him from his dreaming
to an older one   bigger
more lasting   in which he
may return to the ordinariness
and togetherness
that is the unknown

Hands

Alongside each of our minds
your cupped hands
of imagination

hold only
our own two faces

facing each other
in this darkness

I smelt the rest
nervously
an outside world
that tiny fingers   of memory
do not retain

You talk through this world
in a kind of sign language
reeled off like deaf and dumb
on my fingers
without us
even having to hear

I put my words
flat
upturned palms   down
in front of you   for you
to lay yours there   on top

Here in the world
of society
you don't

Your movements are all that I feel

the images   as natural
as if   you are sleeping

Easter Becomes Man

Abstract wanderings, idle speculations
for yesterdays   tomorrows
Let me dig my grave   this Friday
in the darkness of the brown earth

The worms move upwards turning old soil anew
in the passage of mind's slimy digestion

Green pastures on Calvary's hill
with no cross   for me to die on
only the receptive landscape
of my humanity, that smells grace once more

This bread is my earth and this wine my rainfall

unfinished symphony: first movement

the petals turn inwards to this evening's shadow
sighing in cool breezes with whispers like pollen
a tiny star dances to the warmth of a day fallen
on oranges and pinks over deepening green

dream melodies of birdsong surround moments of silence
where leaves nurture hauntings, the voices of shape
like a worm in this solace, past longing escape
i'm wrinkled with ages churning old soil anew

then flowers seem to waver in a misty awareness
of a light in this garden wandering in earth's song
of beeswing and humming and dewdrops that hang on
to the unearthing of a body in the shape of that 'I'

Equinox

A swelling smoke in a storm of leaves
conjures autumn in his brown tears

for see him turn on these broken branches
as the chase has become pursuit
along some other path of stumbling
towards warmth, a fireside

And each glance upwards through trees'
dark winter cracks in a bare sky
sees the year's wounds open

and only the distance of stars shines through

Smugglers

Pressed warm in against another pulse
as a head might hug the ribcage beat
And yet ragged is the word
we'd have to use to describe
the homecoming   the leaves
being abandoned to their fate
the sap following its new plan
down a dark coastline
an occasional smuggling of heat
Don't be fooled by this running
headlong into winter   those leaves
were given something   It came
from that trunk to set them on fire
and reach the ecstasies of a wind
that will take the next breath yet further inside

Dark Tides

Some bodies always seem to be breathing in
unlike the predatory breath

where only the ink black eyeslits lie
above a heavy swell   inwards   and outwards

There the midnight sea
slowly lunges against the land
upon those dark   moonless tides

And the breaking upwards to a seal-skinned surface
only seems to melt heavily over another
in an act of apparent reclamation   Sucking

and pulling the breath downwards
to another earth   long   long below

where the scream is still time away   but coming
and each breath turns just a little bit quicker again for shore

On a Shoreline

The bones remain   half covered
in the earth   Intricately joined
they make a whole backbone
of some long since forgotten animal

A sheep of no real significance
and that shocks me
that significance and intricate design
have got so little in common

And yet I remember her blue eyes
saying   Look at these rocks
Look at that sky
Look   seals

And it's what I can't see
that makes me feel strange

myself

The Ripening Seed

Grey   against the wind

To have let go
would have been
to go with the wind

back to summer
There in the long grass
at the very tip-end of summer

Lying on one elbow
like straw cut
against blue-grey skies
and the certainty of rain

of washing clean the fruit
and finding out its purpose
this multiplicity of flesh

And now your fingers
brown and long
around my wrist
gripping me insistently
down   towards this shelter

a grey stone   space
around a slow fire

Streetwise

Light lies   on the water's surface
as gold-dust might defy
a human law of gravity

or doesn't flow   into the drain
where suspended on black water
a flash of gold
bends over the twisted edge
into darkness
It's a cast-iron system

It's the gutter romance we walk by
sing patter patter
feet fleeting onwards
as if   along a doorstep
          that's uncrossable

where there below
the other side remains
whatever is staggering lightfull
and will only be shaped
by the darkness

Totem Pole

The white moonlit waves
had always mediated
between wind and earth

This place was different

No sea

Just wind
hovering over
the green pine
tree tops
Threatening his roots
so that he'd move on

Sooner or later
he'd try flight
It had to come
sooner   or later

And of course
the first flight
requires power

So he fights it

Till he ignites the dead shavings
of his most wooden
of creations
and slowly sets alight
to his gaze

Now he can see
it's the shadow
that makes it
into the island

Walkabout

A slimy brown round boulder
that shoulders
a waterfall

a column of light-dust suspended
against the green
multiplicity of summer leaf

and a tree somewhere
there behind all that
on the bank

in the darker recesses
of the wood
where the smell is cool

of earth and seems to rise
after rainfall

There our journey waits

for the fruits to fall
and this opening
that will hold them

as moments of light
linger
among the trees

and occasional silence
turns sudden
in the nightfall

All this is in the turning
we have walked down
Now think of it

as the doorway
we turn into

to bring in dawn

Our House

Even with the roof
removed
the windows open
and the floor overgrown
with fresh green meadow

I still sit upright
to marvel
at the smells drifting
from your warm
breathing body

I can't understand
what you did
with all that darkness

so I will wait
and watch over
your dawn

Incidentally

it's our door
that swings night

around day

for sometimes the walls
are like starlight

and sometimes
they disappear
to seem blue

Time

Full Circle

A bright egg yoke

with me standing
like a speck of blood
beneath
its transparent surface

You see

once among time
I sought protection
in the shape
of those edges

It was
my own broken shell

New Year

No thing apparent

though a grey transparency
of something turning

The trace of the old year
not a fuse   but
snail-like and glistening
down the wall of this present

Then here at the foot
something we call fear
till down lower
beneath even those roots

We touch that turning
under cover of expectation

The mud is quiet
our frozen nostrils   full

Historian

I watch you skate
across my imagination
and precariously turn
your half body
to look backwards
two legs struggling to work onwards together
beneath that concentration of grey
hot breath

The breathing never seemed to stop
though history implies something lost

The memories freeze in our minds
the way balance is lost

Twilight

In the beginning

we couldn't read
Whether there was the word
or not
we could only tell
by grunts and caresses

A prod   a moan
a smile even
when the fear had moved over
into shadow
and we stood momentarily
to feel the air

That silhouette against twilight
made an horizon
of us

and our word was born
among starlight
without sound

The Untitled Past

He listens in the night
in dreams

where he can throw his voice

In the morning
in daylight   he tries

When he is alone
he tries to portray the sounds
he heard

as they turned

quivering
beneath the eyelids

in a darkness
of a green of eyes

suddenly
lightfull of night's emptiness

Ghost

The wind is fierce here
Hot dust
stings the eyes

to swirling perceptions
of out there

And the sheer fixedness
of place

creates a delirium

Places are formed
to absorb echoes

The winds move in
and out of the lungs
like a clock

Again

He asks questions
he already knows
the answers to

This will lead him
to a life of qualifications

He'll walk backwards
through each doorway

or let
so many footsteps
pass him by

like on an escalator

This makes him feel
secure

Tomorrow
there is a closed
yellow door
in front of him

There is no key

No handle
or password

And the question he asks now
no longer echoes

At Court

Hush   it's M'lud and he's standing
hollow   his sap deep-rooted
A woman scratches yet again
the more playful side of her head
upsetting my scales of justice
just as we all are seated

A ceremony is in progress I can tell
for only the robes and the villain's scars
act out the drama, in twitches or empty bravado
in a careful adjustment of the status quo

The prisoner's eyes swim with fear, or past anger
arrested into uncontrollable heartbeat
Compassion too emerges from the heart
at a slower rate
along blood-red veins
like those blown across the advocate's face
where shocked nerves have been arrested by alcohol

M'lud's ragged branches are courteously
forgotten, out of some deep-rooted purpose
to do with Springtime it seems to me
and there she goes again, that woman

First Meeting

I know the light green sea pull
of your eyes   I can come there
and feel you offer at least comfort

For in such intimate affairs
as a first meeting
there is no need   but the need felt

and the mystery fully embraced
was the quest you constantly smiled upon

So beneath that pool
        a deepening landscape opens out
and we   within its vast
sand-bottomed silence

must rediscover our own other
selves   while blindly
walking further and further on

to a place we have not been before
though sometimes we look at maps
and sometimes   there's just the laughter
of our forgetting

Leap in the Dark

There is a mysterious dew
a green-flecked circle
round the ebony pool
of each eye

where a million tadpoles cluster
above a surface blistering
in this silt-bottomed pond

And it is all there
beneath the sky   within dark space

There's a turquoise dragon-fly
oh yes   was all in her gaze
when she said look   I see a fish
and I could only just bring myself to surmise

So much energy in that first glimpse
its early morning grass
a mist   and sunrise

But no fish to lurk in my depths
and no surge of purposeful emergence
for there was still the yearning
for some kind of freedom to arise

as if our world
had long forgotten the wink
even before
we saw the twinkle   in the dawn sky

Passages

Passing through your clear-water eyes
as if through a cabinet's
glass front   Autumnal warm
Decadent   earth brown

There on polished wood
you house these two small
loosely draped statues

In their green and whitened bronze
they are as old as Greece
yet gesture and shape
say they've become timeless
in our gaze

The girl lifting her knee
to be poised   and
ready to scatter her feet

while the boy holds a flute
momentarily   in that stillness
lost within fantasy's blood red beat

It is at this moment   father   that I see
you are crying   clearing
the shelves with your great waterfall mind

And tumbling outwards towards my arms
come these two tiny figures   suddenly
which I must now catch   and then somehow house

Corners of Night

In that brightly-lit corner of room

her brown hair was tucked in
round an earlobe   among white of flesh
and sheets   and paintwork still fresh

Only the words were now coloured   in primary
though unspoken shades   within his brain

She would listen then to her breath
for a hint of winter   the dark smell
of hibernation   rising from warm passageways

beneath the whites of their lives

And a pink glow perpetuated the skies
as if the sun had sunk beneath the low ceiling
the mattress become a futon to far-away stars

Her Landscape

By spring her grey eyes
had seen enough snow

The crying had begun

Still grey transparent
falling over her skin
down to salt corners
of an emerging word
or sound

I looked back upwards
at her eyes
in which the year had become awash
without plans spontaneous reflections

and the word bubbling out
long and clear
into cold crisp air
was yes a fragile
dazzling
yes

Spellbound

This woman moves, she becomes still
till she dreams and is everywhere

and I stand in her imagined field
in the middle of a round countryside
succulent green dripping smells
thick with immobility
contradict the bottomless
sense of I
that inhabits my chest

for words don't matter anymore
than she makes them
float
and stream on
outwards
upon this to and fro

Child & Madonna

In her womb he dreamt
of the world   spinning
in the wrong direction

When he got out
perhaps, he would correct
his mistake   He did not wait
long enough   to ask
if it was her dream too

His problem had been how
to communicate

while immersed
in all that water

Anima

The shape is of a flame
flown
beneath a high-
cheek-boned face

Graceful lips   horizontal
corners creeping upwards
to where shadow-leaves
caress hollows
on her cheeks

It has happened before
this vision   the lines
have curved this way
like that
before

A breath grows
in the darkness of my chest

She is the image
I can no longer hold in flesh

A Picture Story

He told her that his mind
was now so cold

She said tell me
in pictures

So he described
the snow
on a hill
beneath the blue sky

and the yellow
daffodil

above the tears

Perhaps now
they could go out
to the movies

Sunday Morning late 20th century

He doesn't seem
to be able
to touch the future

He's caught between
the bath
and getting dressed

He's naked
but no longer wet

In this moment
the steam
has ceased to rise

clean clothes
are just out of reach

He's simply man

And it's her
birthday

Integration

His Landscape

In winter he had kept seeing
that ice-blue sky
as pure
through his new-water eyes

In summer he wanted to wind his way down
through the river's throat

to where columns of light
that hold up that sky

hang motionless
in the flight-paths of insects

a river   in among
all those golds and greens

But here all he sees is brown wood
and brown wood   again and again
hill upon hill

till clouds blowing above these trees
and then over hillsides so long and rolling
that his river would only ever be fed

and tributaries are now many in his mind

Red

There is a man
who opens doors
This is unpopular in winter

He may be said
to have a head full
of too-obvious-to-be-noticed thought

as the sun begins to set
in orange   across blue skies

Instead   it has been said
he may be blind

These colours that he feels
now   include red

As if one view   removed
could hold back
the darkness

At night he is dreaming
among   all those stars

Grey

He has already flown
to the south
in his head

The weather there
is younger

Perhaps it's an affair
where he may recover
the 'sum' of all
he has not yet been

or the knowledge

there will always be
his other
to explore

Here on the outside
the skin flakes

Rain washes away his year

Passing along the gutters
of our minds
he says nothing

The sounds are more like laughter
The nights are always dark

One morning a letter arrives
It's the invitation   to wait

He goes in
Each new winter dawn   breaks

A Looking-Glass War

The lines in this shattered mirror
have taken over
his interest

though he knows
they are simply a spider's web
of blind alleys

Too close for comfort
he blurs those lines
with tears

throws his image
out of focus

Then walking out of himself
he has emerged
looking

Water Rights

He doesn't want to write
sad letters

on the page

He would rather
remember

the more you weep
the less you have to pee

He would rather pass water

These are his water rights

They seep into the earth
like ink
on the day's paper

They show
there

clear messages
in a strange language

This morning he rode an octopus
around the bay

A salt
water dream

An Understanding

He talks
in widening circles
across a still pond

The sounds of geese
somewhere overhead

At night in his dream
a new room is discovered

Two figures appear in it
One different from the other

One only to be seen
in the mirror

The room
has the sound of water in it

A calm wave
gliding its way out
over the surface

The warmth
of his body
listening

Message in a Bottle

Continually fill yourself
with the wide open spaces

Don't let the past fester
or become the future

Let them go
M o o ve

as warm water moves
Ask

as if water asks
Aah

A a a a h
A h a a a a

Biographical note

Colin Kerr spent early years in Glasgow (1949 onwards); then London, Bath, Fife, British Columbia, Lanark and Edinburgh. After briefly studying Electrical Engineering he worked as a sales representative for Ladybird before leaving to study Philosophy and Comparative Religion at Edinburgh University 1974–78.

Since then he has been involved in many local writing groups, edited *Graffiti* Magazine 1984–88, and consistently works on the Writers in Schools scheme in central Scotland.

Presently teaching Religious Education part-time (he defines RE as "The science of passion"); he continues to write, while also training in cross-cultural healing techniques using movement, sound and colour.

"And so this is who I am meant to be..."